WHAT MAKES A MONET A MONET?

Richard Mühlberger

The Metropolitan Museum of Art
Viking
NEW YORK

VIKING
Published by the Penguin Group, Penguin Putnam Books for Young Readers, 345 Hudson Street, New York, New York 10014.

Paperback edition published in 1993 by The Metropolitan Museum of Art and Viking, a division of Penguin Books USA Inc.
Hardcover edition published in 2002 by The Metropolitan Museum of Art and Viking, a division of Penguin Putnam Books for Young Readers.

10 9 8 7 6 5 4 3 2 1

Produced by the Department of Special Publications, The Metropolitan Museum of Art: Series Editor, Mary Beth Brewer; Cover Design, Anna Raff; Design, Nai Y. Chang.

The Library of Congress has cataloged the paperback edition as follows:

Mühlberger, Richard. What makes a Monet a Monet? / Richard Mühlberger.
p. cm.
"The Metropolitan Museum of Art."
Summary: Explores such art topics as style, composition, color, and subject matter as they relate to twelve works by Monet.
ISBN 0-87099-670-3 (MMA pbk.) ISBN 0-670-85200-7 (Viking pbk.)
1. Monet, Claude, 1840–1926—Criticism and interpretation—Juvenile literature. 2. Painting, French—Juvenile literature. 3. Impressionism (Art)—France—Juvenile literature. [1. Monet, Claude, 1840–1926. 2. Painting, French. 3. Art appreciation.] I. Metropolitan Museum of Art (New York, N.Y.) II. Title.
ND553.M7M84 1993 759.4—dc20 93-7583 CIP AC

ISBN 1-58839-050-0 (MMA) ISBN 0-670-03570-X (Viking)

Printed in Italy

ILLUSTRATIONS

Unless otherwise noted, all works are by Claude Monet and in oil on canvas.

Pages 1 and 2: *Bridge over a Pool of Water Lilies*, 36½ x 29 in., 1899, The Metropolitan Museum of Art, H. O. Havemeyer Collection, Bequest of Mrs. H. O. Havemeyer, 1929, 29.100.113.

Page 6: photograph, Claude Monet at age 18, Carjat, Harry N. Abrams, Inc. archives.

Page 8: Eugène Boudin, *On the Beach at Trouville*, oil on wood, 1863, 10 x 18 in., The Metropolitan Museum of Art, Bequest of Amelia B. Lazarus, 1907, 07.88.4.

Page 9: *The Mouth of the Seine at Honfleur*, 35¼ x 59¼ in., 1865, Norton Simon Museum, Pasadena, California, F.1973.33.2.P.

Page 10: *Garden at Sainte-Adresse*, 35⅝ x 51⅛ in., The Metropolitan Museum of Art, Purchased with special contributions and purchase funds given or bequeathed by friends of the Museum, 1967, 67.241.

Page 13: *The Luncheon*, 90½ x 59 in., 1868, Städtische Galerie, Städelsches Kunstinstitut, Frankfurt; photograph, Artothek, Munich.

Page 17: *La Grenouillère*, 29⅜ x 39¼ in., The Metropolitan Museum of Art, H. O. Havemeyer Collection, Bequest of Mrs. H. O. Havemeyer, 1929, 29.100.112.

Page 20: *Impression—Sunrise*, 18⅞ x 24¾ in., 1872, © Musée Marmottan, Paris.

Page 21: Edouard Manet, *Monet Working on His Boat in Argenteuil*, 1874, 32 7/16 x 39 9/16 in., Bayerische Staatsgemäldesammlungen, Munich; photograph, Artothek, Munich.

Page 22: *Poppy Field, Argenteuil*, 21 5/16 x 29 in., 1875, from the Collection of the Hon. and Mrs. Walter H. Annenberg.

Page 24: Edouard Manet, *The Monet Family in Their Garden*, 24 x 39¼ in., The Metropolitan Museum of Art, Bequest of Joan Whitney Payson, 1975, 1976.201.14.

Page 25: *Arrival of the Normandy Train, Saint-Lazare Station*, 23½ x 31⅝ in., 1877, Mr. and Mrs. Martin A. Reyerson Collection, 1933.1158; photograph © 1993, The Art Institute of Chicago. All Rights Reserved.

Page 26: *Gare Saint-Lazare, Arrival of a Train*, 32¾ x 40 in., 1877, Courtesy of The Fogg Art Museum, Harvard University Art Museums, Bequest–Collection of Maurice Wertheim, Class of 1906.

Page 28: *Bouquet of Sunflowers*, 39¾ x 32 in., 1881, The Metropolitan Museum of Art, H. O. Havemeyer Collection, Bequest of Mrs. H. O. Havemeyer, 1929, 29.100.107.

Page 30: *Morning on the Seine near Giverny*, 32⅛ x 36⅝ in., 1897, The Metropolitan Museum of Art, Bequest of Julia W. Emmons, 1956, 56.135.4.

Page 31: *Grainstacks (End of Summer)*, 23⅝ x 39⅜ in., 1891, Arthur M. Wood in memory of Pauline Palmer Wood, 1985.1103; photograph © 1993, The Art Institute of Chicago. All Rights Reserved.

Pages 32–33: *Haystacks (Effect of Snow and Sun)*, 25¾ x 36¼ in., 1891, The Metropolitan Museum of Art, H. O. Havemeyer Collection, Bequest of Mrs. H. O. Havemeyer, 1929, 29.100.109.

Page 34: *Poplars*, 32¼ x 32⅛ in., The Metropolitan Museum of Art, H. O. Havemeyer Collection, Bequest of Mrs. H. O. Havemeyer, 1929, 29.100.110.

Page 36: *Rouen Cathedral: The Portal (In Sun)*, 39¼ x 25⅞ in., 1894, The Metropolitan Museum of Art, Theodore M. Davis Collection, Bequest of Theodore M. Davis, 1915, 30.95.250; photograph, Malcolm Varon.

Page 37: photograph, Rouen Cathedral, Bertrand de Chauvigny and Patty Lurie.

Page 38: *Rouen Cathedral (Early Morning)*, 39¼ x 25½ in., 1894, Museum Folkwang Essen.

Page 38: *Rouen Cathedral (Early Afternoon)*, oil on linen, 39½ x 26 in., 1894, Chester Dale Collection, © 1993 National Gallery of Art, Washington.

Page 39: *Rouen Cathedral (Early Evening)*, 39⅜ x 25⅝ in., 1892, © Musée Marmottan, Paris.

Page 39: *Rouen Cathedral (Evening)*, 39⅜ x 25⅝ in., National Museum of Wales, Cardiff.

Page 41: *Bridge over a Pool of Water Lilies*, 36½ x 29 in., 1899, The Metropolitan Museum of Art, H. O. Havemeyer Collection, Bequest of Mrs. H. O. Havemeyer, 1929, 29.100.113.

Page 41: Utagawa Hiroshige, *Inside Kameido Tenjin Shrine*, from the series *One Hundred Famous Views of Edo*, color woodblock print, 14¼ x 9¾ in., 1856, The Metropolitan Museum of Art, The Howard Mansfield Collection, Purchase, Rogers Fund, 1936, JP 2517.

Page 42: *The Houses of Parliament (Effect of Fog)*, 32 x 36⅜ in., The Metropolitan Museum of Art, Bequest of Julia W. Emmons, 1956, 56.135.6.

Pages 44–45: *Water Lilies*, 39¾ x 78¾ in., 1919, from the Collection of the Hon. and Mrs. Walter H. Annenberg.

Page 47: photograph, Monet in front of his *Water Lilies* in his studio at Giverny, Roger-Viollet, Paris.

Page 49: *Red Boats, Argenteuil*, 24⅜ x 32½ in., 1875, Courtesy of The Fogg Art Museum, Harvard University Art Museums, Bequest–Collection of Maurice Wertheim, Class of 1906.

CONTENTS

MEET CLAUDE MONET 7

GARDEN AT SAINTE-ADRESSE 10

THE LUNCHEON 13

LA GRENOUILLÈRE 16

POPPY FIELD, ARGENTEUIL 23

GARE SAINT-LAZARE 25

BOUQUET OF SUNFLOWERS 29

HAYSTACKS 31

POPLARS 34

ROUEN CATHEDRAL 37

BRIDGE OVER A POOL OF WATER LILIES 40

THE HOUSES OF PARLIAMENT 43

WATER LILIES 44

WHAT MAKES A MONET A MONET? 48

The year this photograph was taken of the dashing 18-year-old Monet, an oil painting by him was exhibited in the annual exhibition at Le Havre. It was the start of a new career for the very self-confident-looking young man. Although he may not appear to be one, Monet was already a rebel and would have difficult years ahead making a living from his paintings.

Meet Claude Monet

Oscar-Claude Monet was born in Paris, France, on November 14, 1840. When he was five years old, his family moved to the seaside city of Le Havre. He went to school there, but he was not much of a student. He liked to draw irreverent caricatures of his teachers, who tried in vain to get him to concentrate on other subjects. Monet later confessed that he did not learn much in school except some spelling. "It seemed like a prison, and I could never bear to stay there, even for four hours a day, especially when the sunshine beckoned and the sea was smooth," he said.

Monet's favorite activity was wandering along the beaches, making caricatures of tourists. He usually pictured a person with a very small body and a very large head, exaggerating the nose or some other part of the face. He sold his caricatures for ten to twenty francs, more than what his teachers earned in a day! By the time Monet was fifteen years old, a local art-supply shop had begun to exhibit his caricatures in its window. After that, many people began to place orders for humorous portraits of themselves by the young artist.

Seeing What Painting Could Be

The works of a painter named Eugène Boudin were sometimes shown in the shop window, too. Boudin kept track of anyone else's work that appeared there. Seeing that Monet had an observant eye, he asked the teenager to go painting with him, but Monet did not want to be a painter and steered away from Boudin. The day he finally saw Boudin at work, however, Monet changed his mind. "Suddenly, a veil was removed" from his eyes, he recalled, and he realized "what painting could be." From then on, he often accompanied the older artist on outdoor painting excursions.

At that time, painting outdoors was considered unartistic. The art schools trained students to paint in their studios. They also taught them to mine subjects from history and myth. But Boudin showed Monet that these rules, and many others, were ridiculous. Together they stalked landscape subjects and tried to paint exactly what they saw. Boudin liked to capture a scene on his canvas just as it was when he first saw it, not later, in a studio. The initial impression was special to him. Monet easily imitated Boudin because drawing caricatures had given him practice in capturing images quickly. But because Boudin insisted on being true to nature, Monet could no longer exaggerate what he saw. When he was seventeen, one of his paintings was shown in an art exhibition sponsored by the city of Le Havre. It was a landscape of the place where he and Boudin had gone on their first painting excursion.

The French Impressionists

During the next eight years, Monet studied in Paris, served in the army, painted almost constantly, and met many artists. Among his new friends were Pierre-Auguste Renoir, Camille Pissarro, Alfred Sisley, and Jean-Frédéric Bazille. All of them wanted to paint life as it was, seizing a fleeting moment, capturing the first instant of seeing a subject. By painting outdoors, on the spot and quickly, they learned to make pictures that were fresh and full of atmosphere. Their secret—if there was a secret—was not to concentrate on the colors of the landscape until they had first pinned down the color of the daylight. Was it gray, gold, pink, or blue? Once they knew that, the other colors came easily and gloriously. These painters became the French

Eugène Boudin
ON THE BEACH AT TROUVILLE

Sky is often prominent in Boudin's canvases, taking up far more space than sea and low-lying sand. The son of a sailor, Boudin was impatient indoors and was one of the first artists to master painting outdoors. Monet said that by Boudin's example, "My destiny as a painter opened out to me."

Impressionists, one of the most famous groups of artists in history. Other French painters joined them in their break from tradition. Then Americans came to learn about Impressionism, and Spaniards and Italians followed. Monet was adored as their leader, a position he never wanted. He even refused honors from the French government. What was important to him throughout the seventy years that he painted was to honor the lessons of his master, Boudin. He did this by never abandoning the passion Boudin had inspired in him for painting the outdoors. With fresh canvases under his arm and a paint box and easel strapped to his back, Monet returned again and again to the coastal sites where he and Boudin had painted together, even after he became a famous artist.

In Love with the Sea

Monet was in love with the sea. He said that he always wanted to be "near it or on it." As a boy, he climbed the ocean cliffs and followed their rugged paths along the coast near the busy port city where his family lived. By the time he discovered his career as a painter, he knew every jetty and beach in the district. His earliest paintings were of these familiar scenes. A harbor view and a painting of the coast at low tide earned him his first recognition in the huge annual art exhibition in Paris known as the Salon. In these two beautiful paintings, Monet showed the rawness and danger of nature, depicting the sea the way a fisherman who had suffered through storms might view it.

THE MOUTH OF THE SEINE AT HONFLEUR

Monet's name became known beyond his small circle of friends when a popular art journal praised this painting, one of the two Monet first exhibited in the Salon. Monet's "audacious manner of seeing things" and his sensitivity to color were among the accomplishments singled out for comment. One kind critic said that Monet's The Mouth of the Seine at Honfleur "brought us to an abrupt halt, and we shall never forget it."

Garden at Sainte-Adresse

In *Garden at Sainte-Adresse*, Monet captured a different sea, the comfortable one that formed the backdrop of his family's social life. Monet's father dominates the scene. He sits solidly in his bentwood chair, staring out at the harbor. His commanding posture and his concentration almost transform the terrace into a ship, and him into the ship's captain.

"Captain" Monet's Nautical Eye

Art lovers of 1867 were perplexed by Monet's composition. They could not understand why he had pushed the terrace off center. They insisted that the position of the two flagpoles proved that the artist's vision was skewed. But if Monet had turned more to his left, centering everything, the red, white, and blue flag of France would have flapped against the picture frame. Another important reason for Monet's asymmetrical arrangement was to provide ample space around the figure of his father. This was not because he wanted the man to appear to be alone, but because Monet had a daring idea in mind for the design of the painting.

The scene is filled with strong vertical and horizontal lines. The blue-green horizon and the top of the brown railing are the dominant horizontal elements. The flagpoles, the two standing figures, the red gladiolus, and the masts of the ships are the vertical accents. To make the painting lively, Monet needed a powerful diagonal line to cut through the rigid framework he had built. Nothing gentle would do. He positioned his father to achieve this breakthrough. Old Mr. Monet's stare establishes the diagonal line his son was looking for. It is reinforced by the shadow of his body and the chair next to him. This imaginary line cuts across the terrace, the flagpole, the railing, and on out to the farthest ship entering the harbor. Monet's "skewed" composition is thus balanced by "captain" Monet's nautical eye.

A Garden of Colorful Dots

Monet painted everything on the terrace to look real, so the terrace itself appears to be flat, extending toward the water as it would if seen in real life. In contrast, he represented the sea in a shorthand way, painting dark wavelike lines over a lighter background color. Lacking the shadings of the real ocean, it seems like a flat, painted backdrop for a play on a stage.

The flower garden rises above the terrace on the left side of the painting. Next to Monet's father sits the artist's aunt Sophie, with her parasol blocking the back of her head. The parasol's rounded shape is repeated in the backs and arms of the chairs and the flower bed that separates her from the couple who talk so intently at the water's edge. The luxuriant border that encloses the terrace starts directly behind Aunt Sophie, and her cream-colored suit

stands out from the dots of bright red, yellow, and green all around her.

Starting Out Poor

Monet did not earn enough money from the sale of his paintings to support himself. His poverty forced him to live for a year with his aunt in her weekend house at Sainte-Adresse. She gave him her attic studio, but he never used it. He tramped the beaches to find subjects and painted them then and there.

Although Monet's economic situation changed much for the better in the years ahead, many of his interests remained the same. Flowers and water were two of his favorite subjects for the next sixty years.

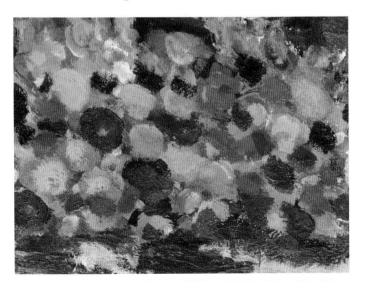

The Luncheon

In 1868, Monet rented a cottage near the sea and settled down to family life with Camille, his frequent model, and their son, Jean. His painting *The Luncheon* shows a warm, domestic scene.

In this work, Monet gives the inviting impression that the empty place at the table is set for the person who is viewing the painting. At such close range, only a few glances are necessary to take in everything. Attention is first drawn to the sunshine-flooded table. A fast inspection finds bowls, dishes, bottles, and cruets of appetizing food and drink. Next, the eyes rise to greet the seated woman and the baby and the woman standing beside the window. A final look takes in the floor.

The Heart of the Painting

In *Garden at Sainte-Adresse*, Monet carefully positioned his father to create the strong diagonal that his painting needed. Here his paternal pride leads him to use similar compositional devices to make little Jean, his one-year-old son, the center of attention, even though the boy is far from the center of the canvas. The guest, who has not yet lifted her veil or removed her gray gloves, leans in a relaxed way against the windowsill. Monet made her conspicuous. She is taller than the seated figures, the left side of the tablecloth angles up to her, and the loaf of bread that sits precariously on

eggs, crusty bread, a leafy salad with oil and vinegar, salami and crackers, a bowl of jam, and red wine with water to wash it down.

Two books are stacked on the side table, a sign that Claude and Camille took time to keep up with the latest authors, some of whom they knew. Jean's broken doll, the colorful ball on the floor, and the wrinkled tablecloth are signs that in Monet's household other things were more important than being tidy and well pressed.

Monet did not intend the public to know that this was his family. He wanted Jean, Camille, the maid, and the visitor to represent modern life, a subject very popular with writers at the time. Many young artists were seeking to capture in paint what these writers had described with words. The title Monet chose for his painting, *The Luncheon*, was a very familiar term, and all the dining room details were familiar, too. Middle-class people could accept the scene as something they knew. "Ah, yes," they might say, "that's just how it is at my house."

the edge of the table points right at her. But any attention she receives, she diverts to the child by quietly looking toward him with downcast eyes. Camille, his mother, also looks at the little boy. Her face, in profile, focuses on his energetic spoon pounding, and she wraps one arm around his shoulders. Even the tablecloth urges the viewer to look at the impatient child. The rough white linen seems to run into his white napkin, and he is the only one who seems ready and eager to eat.

A Farmer's Meal
With a little money in his pocket, Monet had hired a maid to help Camille around the house so she could concentrate on raising their son. Although this may seem extravagant for a poor artist, the food on the table proves that Monet's needs remained simple and basic—soft-boiled

La Grenouillère

Monet liked to be close to Paris. It was the best place for him to show and sell his paintings, so he moved his family to a country town on the river Seine just outside the great capital city. His good friend from art school days, Pierre-Auguste Renoir, joined him on painting excursions to a place popular for weekend outings called La Grenouillère, which means "frog pond." It was on an island in the river Seine not far from Monet's rented house.

The "Frog Pond"

Monet and Renoir painted side by side with their toes almost in the water. Monet made the little round island the hub of his painting, with catwalks, bathers, and boats radiating out from it. The roof of the floating boat-rental pavilion on the right protects customers from the sun. One of the clients, top hat in place, maneuvers the narrow plank to the tree-shaded islet. On the left, swimmers stand in water barely up to their shoulders, the women garbed in black from their ankles to their necks, and the men stripped to their waists. A second catwalk leads past rental boats to the shore. Monet lavished most of his attention on his great love, the water. It is as much the subject of the painting as the people, the island, the pavilion, and the boats.

A Gift for Painting Water

The Seine laps gently against the shore and the floating pavilion, boats swaying in its wake. Sun shines down onto the broken surface of the river. Dark, vigorous dashes of paint indicate the reflections of the trees on the water. Glittering white brushstrokes indicate sunshine. At the bottom of the painting, all of these freely painted strokes are wide. Moving backward, they gradually become narrower to indicate distance. Closer to the shoreline, longer strokes of green, blue, and pink show the water lapping toward land. While the water ripples in the foreground, it flows in the background. Monet's contemporary, the great French novelist Emile Zola, described Monet's gift for painting water. "With him," Zola wrote, "water is alive, profound, and above all, real."

Sailboats were popular at La Grenouillère, but Monet showed only rowboats. The patterns of sky showing through the trees on the opposite shore, however, resemble sails and bring movement to that corner of the painting.

The trees in the background are painted with quick, wide brushstrokes of green. The darker leaves that cascade from the branches on the left and the foliage of the lone tree on the islet are done with short, energetic brushstrokes.

The figures, too, are created in a shorthand way. With a half dozen or so moves of the brush, Monet indicated the shape and bend of each body. The two women on the islet in black bathing costumes were not given faces. By their postures, however, Monet indicated that the one on the left is timid of the water, and that the other is curious to know what the swimmer holds in his hands.

Monet cropped, or cut off, the rowboat on the right side of the painting, but he did not ignore its jaunty red stripes. He painted them twice—first on the boat itself, then reflected in the rippling water. The rosy-colored zigzags stand out against the darkest section of water and look as though they are constantly moving.

1. Patterns of the sky
2. Wide, loose brushstrokes
3. Shorter brushstrokes
4. Simplified figures
5. Rowboat and its reflections

The Sketch Is a Painting

Monet first thought of his painting of La Grenouillère as a sketch. He made a few others, showing different angles of the same scene. He planned to refer to them in creating a larger painting for the Salon, but this never came about. Perhaps he realized that his "sketch" was a satisfying, complete work of art in itself.

The Salon valued grand canvases based on historical events, subjects that never interested Monet. Scenes from everyday life, which he liked to paint, were considered of minor importance. Monet came to realize that the size of a painting did not matter any more than painting the past, and he made an important break with the way art had been practiced for hundreds of years. He relished working on a more intimate scale, re-creating what he saw around him.

The Birth of Impressionism

It is said that when Monet and Renoir painted these fresh and spontaneous canvases of modern life, La Grenouillère witnessed the birth of Impressionism. Although he did not mean to, Monet gave the name to the new movement. In 1874, when thirty rebellious artists decided to show their work together, one of Monet's contributions to the exhibition was called

IMPRESSION—SUNRISE

Hoping to sell paintings, Monet and his friends decided to exhibit their works together. Their first group exhibition was held in 1874. A journalist made fun of Monet's painting Impression—Sunrise, *stating that it was only an impression. His words implied that it was not a complete painting. In spite of the insult, the style of the young artists now had a name, Impressionism.*

Impression—Sunrise. A critic ridiculed the title and the painting, but the word "Impressionist" soon became a badge of honor. Many of the original artists dropped out, but a smaller group exhibited together seven more times, disbanding in 1886. Monet's innovative way of painting led to his frequent exclusion from official Salon exhibitions for years.

A Floating Studio

Monet moved many times during his early years, living with friends, in hotel rooms, or in other rented quarters. In 1871, he rented a house for his family in Argenteuil, a small town on the Seine about fifteen minutes by train from Paris. The town was famous for its regatta, and boating enthusiasts flocked there on weekends and during the summer. Monet had the oddest boat of all, a small floating studio that one of his neighbors helped him build soon after he settled into his new home. It was a broad rowboat equipped with a shed where he kept canvases and other painting supplies and where his wife, Camille, sometimes sat to keep out of the sun. There was room for Monet and his easel under a striped awning.

Edouard Manet
MONET WORKING ON HIS BOAT IN ARGENTEUIL

The modern painter most esteemed by the Impressionists was Edouard Manet, yet he refused to exhibit with his admirers, seeking official recognition instead. By 1874, the year he painted this picture of Monet under the awning of his floating studio, Manet was working in the sun-speckled style of the Impressionists.

Poppy Field, Argenteuil

It was probably in his peculiar boat that Monet rowed across the river with his eight-year-old son Jean to paint a gorgeous field of wild flowers located near the shore.

A Rainbow of Paint

Planting his easel in the middle of nature's garden, Monet painted an idyllic scene. In it, a silvery segment of the Seine can be spied between the two small poplar trees on the far left. The clouds that scud along the horizon and billow higher into the sky are lined with lavender. Under them, a long, gently curving avenue flourishes with bright red poppies, flaming salvia, sage, lavender, and other flowers that grow to the height of young Jean's waist. A straw hat shades the boy's face from the sun. Jean was the focus of *The Luncheon*, but here is simply part of the landscape. To picture the sheer beauty and richness of the scene before him, Monet applied a rainbow of paint in flickering strokes and dabs.

Using Color to Compose

Far back in the painting, bright splashes of yellow sunlight fall across the fields like banners of silk. This stretch of yellow does more than help describe the kind of day it is. It doubles the thickness of the horizontal line made by the distant hills, adding enough weight to the composition across the right side so that the two hefty trees will not tip it to the left. Patches of rose in the lower right quarter of the canvas also aid in this balance, for red always steps forward from the colors around it. By catching the viewer's eye, the bright poppies prevent the trees from being the focus of the painting. Instead, the theme seems to be a special moment when the great expanse of cloud-filled sky meets the

When he painted La Grenouillère, Monet applied broad slashes with his paintbrush to capture the appearance of the water. In Poppy Field, Argenteuil, he applied dabs as well as dashes. Each deft flick of his brush against the canvas defined another small flower or cluster of leaves.

almost endless extent of the colorful fields. The slanted lines of the field and the height of the poplar trees are what make this happen.

If young Jean had looked over his father's shoulder before the canvas was finished, he would not have found even one section done. Monet did not paint the sky first, then the trees, then the foreground, finishing one section after the other. That was the old way. He began by quickly filling the entire canvas with the right tones, dabbing color everywhere until recognizable shapes emerged. Details were finally flicked on, and it then seemed as though all the sections of the canvas came into focus simultaneously.

Other painters were also attracted to Argenteuil. Manet lived not far from the poppy fields. Renoir, Sisley, and Berthe Morisot enjoyed the variety of views offered by the town and its surroundings, and they visited it frequently. While there, they all painted airy, colorful pictures full of optimism and happiness.

"Five or Six Lunatics"

Although today it is said that Impressionism reached its peak during the 1870s at Argenteuil, at the time the public hated everything the Impressionists did. The press greeted exhibitions of their paintings with sarcasm. One critic wrote, "Five or six lunatics . . . have joined to show their work." The few pictures Monet sold were to other artists or their friends. For years, he had an income only because his dealer bought paintings from him, even though the dealer had no customers for the canvases. All of this was to change, but it took ten more years before there was acceptance of Monet's paintings.

Edouard Manet
THE MONET FAMILY IN THEIR GARDEN

Manet here pictured Monet gardening while Camille and Jean laze nearby. Before Manet was done, Monet took up a canvas and painted a picture of Manet painting this picture. All the while, another famous painter was there, ignoring his artist friends in order to paint a double portrait of Camille and Jean. He was Renoir. All of them, and many others, enjoyed painting at Argenteuil.

Gare Saint-Lazare

"Last Stop—Gare Saint-Lazare"

The first steam-powered railroad train in France chugged between just two provincial cities in 1832. Thirteen years later, by the time Monet's family moved to Le Havre, almost five thousand steam engines linked every part of the country with Paris. Critics complained that the tracks and the soot-belching engines spoiled the countryside, but many people prized locomotives. Trains allowed weekend jaunts with family or friends and made it easy to visit distant relatives. A train whisked Monet from the village station at Argenteuil to the bustle of Gare Saint-Lazare whenever he needed to be in Paris. He and his comrades painted trains as beautiful features of the landscape. In January of 1877, Monet decided to picture them under the modern glass-and-iron roof of the Paris station.

Comical or Magnificent?

With the help of a wealthy artist friend, Monet rented a studio near Gare Saint-Lazare. For the next three months he painted nothing but the station, the neighborhood around it, and trains coming and going. By April, he had finished a dozen or more canvases, and seven of them were shown at an Impressionist exhibition. It was the third time in three years that the Impressionists had exhibited their work together. The earlier shows had been criticized by the newspapers, and this time a comic play was even written about the exhibition. In it, an Impressionist turns his painting every which way, never able to tell what the subject is. Another writer, this one friendly to the Impressionists, called Monet's Gare Saint-Lazare paintings "magnificent." Looking at one, he wrote that it "arouses the same emotion that nature would, but more strongly perhaps because the artist's emotion is also apparent in the painting."

ARRIVAL OF THE NORMANDY TRAIN, SAINT-LAZARE STATION

GARE SAINT-LAZARE, ARRIVAL OF A TRAIN

Painting Billowing Steam

In this painting of Gare Saint-Lazare, the dreary, blue-gray winter sky cloaks the large building in the background. The locomotive steam that funnels to the heights of the station is the same color as the sky, but darker. Light passing through the glass of the ceiling spills touches of color onto the ruddy ground between the tracks. The billowing steam, the most transient of all the things Monet saw, fills the middle and the upper half of the canvas.

In his painting, Monet played round shapes against rectangular ones. The tracks, the ceiling, and the trains direct the eye toward the hazy city scene outside the station. But the white puffs of smoke in the middle of the tracks, floating like bunches of balloons, halt this exit. They bring the viewer back into the picture with the arriving train.

Making Wild Parties Out of the Rainbow

Again and again, when Monet returned to the station he discovered that its colors changed with the time of day and the weather. He reached for different colors with each canvas he painted. In this one blue is dominant, in another, yellow, and in still another, lavender. Although the station remained the same and the locomotives that came and went looked alike, each painting is unique.

On seeing the Gare Saint-Lazare paintings, one critic accused Monet of "making wild parties out of the rainbow." He was struck much more by the colors than the station. This would have pleased Monet, who saw the colors of the things he painted before anything else. The group of Gare Saint-Lazare canvases was the first of many series that Monet painted during his long lifetime. Each of the series concentrated on a single subject, or motif.

Colors have opposites, called complements. The complement of yellow is violet, and the complement of orange is blue. Red and green are complements, too. Placed next to one another, complementary colors vibrate. Here Monet used their power, placing the bright yellow and orange flowers against a violet and blue backdrop. Similarly, he placed a red tablecloth beneath the rich green leaves. Monet frequently made use of complementary colors.

Bouquet of Sunflowers

Monet liked to be outdoors and did most of his painting in the open air, but when he was housebound, he painted whatever was at hand. His subjects ranged from his own paint box to an uncooked beef roast. In 1879, his wife, Camille, died, and by 1881, he became foster father to a new family. Now when he stayed indoors, he was surrounded by eight exuberant children. A series of equally lively flower pieces resulted.

In 1878, helped by his friends, Monet had rented a big house in the village of Vétheuil on a bend of the river Seine, more than two hours by train to Gare Saint-Lazare. He tended a flower garden there, its wide stairs and a path cutting through the colorful plantings flanked by rows of sunflowers. This painting shows a bunch in a Japanese porcelain vase, which rests on a table covered with a fringed square of red silk.

Off Center Is More Interesting

Monet could have placed the vase in the middle of the painting, but he decided it would look more interesting slightly off center. Because the vase is to the right of the central axis, two flowers on the right butt against the frame. On the left, one blossom stretches to touch the edge of the canvas. The flowers that don't stretch out nestle into the foliage. With leaves descending and blossoms pushing out or shrinking in, the bouquet is a glowing center of energy.

To create his sunflowers, Monet painted short strokes of orange, yellow, and brown, laying one color over another. Longer, curving brushstrokes indicated the drooping leaves. They consist of different shades of green, one of which is nearly black. Up close to the flowers while he painted, Monet noticed every detail, but used the same strong brushstrokes that are seen in his outdoor paintings.

A Home in Giverny

As Monet approached the middle of his life, he could count more than two dozen different places where he had lived. The time spent with his new, extended family must have inspired him to settle down, for in 1883 he rented the house where he was to spend the next half of his life. It was in Giverny, forty miles from Paris. He liked it because it was near water, there were schools down the road for the children, and there was a flowering orchard on the property. After he found the house, he quickly wrote to his dealer, "Once settled, I hope to produce masterpieces."

At Giverny, Monet's art changed. In the past, he had frequently selected popular subjects of the day, slices of modern life. But at Giverny, modern things and activities of the middle class no longer attracted him. He abandoned subjects like those in *The Luncheon, La Grenouillère,* and the Gare Saint-Lazare series. He became more possessed than ever by the fleeting nature of what he saw. The painter Paul Cézanne, one of Monet's famous contemporaries, described him as "only an eye," a mild insult meaning that Monet painted what he saw, but did not think about it. While Cézanne expected more from an artist, he quickly added words of admiration for

Monet: "But what an eye!"

Monet purchased the house and land he had been renting in Giverny in 1890. The two-story pink stucco building with green shutters is located on a small branch of the river Seine called the Ru. A second tributary, the Epte, snakes its way through the fields nearby. One of Monet's stepdaughters, Blanche, took up art and became his assistant. Together they went on many painting excursions.

MORNING ON THE SEINE NEAR GIVERNY

Haystacks

Harvest scenes that glorified ordinary field workers became popular during Monet's youth. Haystacks symbolized the dignity of labor and even religious and political ideas. None of this motivated Monet. He painted haystacks because they were nearby and because he liked the sheen of the straw and the shape of the piles.

Hunting for an Impression

Monet had first painted haystacks in 1888, but it wasn't until 1890 that he began to concentrate on them. A French writer, Guy de Maupassant, watched Monet paint, and described how the artist captured his impressions. "Actually, he was no longer a painter," he wrote, "but a hunter."

The writer said that Monet usually had five or six canvases, all incomplete, "depicting the same subject at different hours of the day and with different effects." Monet "waited, watched the sun and the shadows, capturing in a few brushstrokes a falling ray of light, or a passing cloud . . . ." Blanche good-heartedly said that for many months she was in charge of a wheelbarrow, carrying "as many canvases as there were different impressions to seize." Monet's one complaint was, "The sun sets so fast that I cannot follow it." He was seeking "the instant," so Blanche had to be very quick in getting out the right canvas whenever the light changed.

Winter came and the farmer who owned the

GRAINSTACKS (END OF SUMMER)
In 1891, Monet exhibited fifteen of the haystack pictures. Viewers were amazed by the changes of light and atmosphere he captured in each. Here Monet explored the warmth of the summer sun.

field wanted to remove the haystacks. Monet paid him to leave them alone until he completed his series. He painted them in all kinds of weather, but he particularly liked their appearance in the coldest months. Many of his haystack paintings are snow scenes.

Using "Negative" Space

In this painting, the two haystacks overlap, their edges making a **V** the same size as the small haystack. The **V** is not just a space, but a shape—a negative shape, in art terminology. It keeps the left side of the composition from becoming too heavy. By giving the small haystack a phantom partner, Monet doubled its visual weight and balanced the composition. Years of practice gave the artist an instinct for placing shapes in just the right spots. His **V** marks the center of the painting.

Although Monet claimed that painting the haystacks was "continual torture," the finished works were a success when they were exhibited in Paris. Fifteen were shown together, as Monet intended that they be seen, and in three days every one of them was sold. An enthusiastic critic called Monet a poet, and American artists began to visit him to learn about Impressionism. Monet soon returned to the fields to paint more haystacks. They were a favorite subject of his for two more years.

HAYSTACKS (EFFECT OF SNOW AND SUN)

Poplars

Seven-Minute Impressions

A row of poplar trees grew along the meandering Epte River near Monet's home. At about the time he started his series of haystacks, he began painting these trees. Rising straight and high into the sky and reflected by the water below, the poplars gave Monet ideas for canvases that were strikingly different from those of the squat and earthy haystacks. One admirer called the new paintings "the whirl series."

In this painting, four tree trunks fill the square canvas. Distant trees, painted in yellow, are seen on the left. Everything is mirrored in the still and clear river, and it is easy to confuse sky with water and the trees and plants with their reflections. Monet chose a spot where the trees were neither perfectly straight nor quite evenly spaced, for he enjoyed the slight variations this brought to his composition. He framed his scene dramatically. The tops of the trees are cut off, as are most of their reflections in the water below.

An American who spent summers in Giverny recalled that these canvases ". . .were painted from a broad-bottomed boat fitted up with grooves to hold a number of canvases. He [Monet] told me that in one of his [Poplars] the effect lasted only seven minutes, or until the sunlight left a certain leaf, when he took out the next canvas and worked on that."

"It's Finished"

While Monet was painting his poplar series, he learned that the trees were to be cut down and auctioned for lumber. He asked the mayor of the town to let him finish his paintings first, but was told that nothing could be done. Monet cleverly went to the owner of a local lumberyard who

wanted the trees, persuading him to bid high for them at the auction. Monet promised to pay the difference between the man's winning bid, no matter how high, and what the trees were really worth. The lumberman agreed, and the trees were not felled until Monet had completed his series of paintings.

Monet worked on several paintings at a time, switching canvases as the day's colors changed. It was difficult to capture an impression. When the sun went behind a cloud, the colors of leaves, water, and sky all changed. If a morning mist made a scene appealing to Monet, the scene was different the instant the mist evaporated. The blue tones of a chilly morning quickly became yellow or orange as the sun warmed the day. So Monet was slow to say, "It's finished." He must have felt that another day would bring the perfect impression to help him really finish a canvas. He stored paintings in his large studio, and he did not sign them until they were about to go to an exhibition or were sold. His signature was a simple "Claude Monet" in the lower corner of the canvas. One of the artist's stepsons reported that when Monet signed a painting, he often added more color, too, recalling a particular moment of a particular day when he first painted it.

As the Epte River flows through the flat countryside, the poplars along its shore can be seen between the poplars in the foreground. This close-up shows how Monet suggested those distant forms with yellow, green, and lavender strokes over pink and white paint. Red accents capture the jewellike glow of the poplar leaves in the evening sun. Layers of purple and lavender over light and dark green represent the scrubby shrubbery along the river's bank. These colors blend in the viewer's eye.

ROUEN CATHEDRAL: THE PORTAL (IN SUN)

From Rouen, Monet wrote to his wife, "What terrible weather! And how changing it is!. . . Good Lord, how difficult it is to do this Cathedral! Tomorrow it will be eight days since I have been here, and I have been working every day on the two same canvases and yet have been unable to achieve what I wanted."

Rouen Cathedral

The winter of 1892 was too cold for the fifty-two-year-old Monet to trek across frozen fields to paint scenes near his home in Giverny. Instead, he decided to paint the Cathedral of Notre-Dame in the nearby city of Rouen, something he had wanted to do for a long time. Many of Monet's painting excursions up and down the Seine and to the coastal towns he loved so much took him through Rouen. He knew the city and its architecture well. He was in luck and found a room with a big window directly across from the church. For the first time, the artist was going to paint an outdoor scene from indoors.

The construction of Rouen's Cathedral of Notre-Dame began in the year 1202 and progressed through the lifetimes of many stonecutters and stonemasons. By the time it was completed, more than two hundred years later, its facade was one of the most ornate in France, with four towers, dozens of arches, carved figures of saints, and a huge, round window over the entrance.

Monument and Mirage

Little sky and almost no ground show in Monet's painting. He was so close to the cathedral that he could see no more of it from his room. One large tower on the right was out of his range entirely, and the tops of the other towers soared

Monet's vantage point from a second-floor window across the street from the church cut off the tops of the towers, the building's most admired features. But Monet was more interested in the magic that light performed on the ancient stones, changing their colors day by day, and even minute by minute.

beyond the frame of his window. More of the subject is omitted, but not because of Monet's station on the second floor. The tan limestone of the church reflected the brilliant winter sunlight so strongly that Monet could not see details of the sculptures or the architectural carvings.

The building's vertical piers and windows and the pointed arches, linked together by a few horizontals, are like a skeleton or frame reaching upward. Everything else appears to be on the verge of melting around these props. Because the longest lines on either side of the main doors slant slightly, the upper part of the cathedral appears to lean backward. In his paintings, Monet pictured the impressive old building as

ROUEN CATHEDRAL, EARLY MORNING

ROUEN CATHEDRAL, EARLY AFTERNOON

a great stone monument, and at the same time as an insubstantial mirage.

Monet returned to Rouen during the winter of the following year and brought all of his unfinished cathedral paintings with him. Again he watched how weather and light changed the color of the church's stone. When atmospheric conditions matched what was on a particular canvas, that was the painting on which he worked. Monet wrote to his wife, "Each day I add and subtract something that I had not even known how to see before." Perhaps because he was used to the freedom of painting outdoors, he became frustrated at the difficulty of painting the cathedral. He considered abandoning the canvases, but instead brought them all back to

ROUEN CATHEDRAL, EARLY EVENING

ROUEN CATHEDRAL, EVENING

Giverny. Too busy to return to Rouen for a third painting session, he completed the works from memory. For the first time, Monet abandoned the primary rule of his mentor, Boudin, to paint exactly what he saw when and where he saw it. Monet said, "The further I go, the more difficulty I have rendering what I feel; . . . anyone who claims to have finished a picture is terribly conceited." He immediately sold four of the paintings for a record price. Twenty more were exhibited in 1895 in Paris. Georges Clemenceau, the most famous statesman in France, wrote that Monet "has given us the feeling that he could have, should have, made fifty, one hundred, a thousand paintings, as many as he had seconds in his life."

Bridge over a Pool of Water Lilies

Getting to Know a New Landscape

Monet spent many years at Giverny planning and planting a splendid garden between his pink house and the quiet road that passed it. In 1893, he purchased the property on the other side of the house, across the railroad tracks. Along one of its boundaries flowed the narrow Ru River. The new land featured a small lily pond, which Monet envisioned as an elaborate water garden. The shallow pool was excavated to make it larger, the little river was diverted to feed it, and dozens of trees, water-loving flowers, and flowering shrubs were planted around it. But all of these handsome, rare, and exotic plants became

In painting the water lilies, Monet wove together a rich web of color. His brushstrokes are made up not only of green, but of yellow, pink, red, white, lavender, and blue.

mere foils for the water lilies. At first, Monet did not paint them often. "It always takes a while to get to know a new landscape," he said. But eventually, he greatly expanded the pool and painted almost nothing but the water lilies. They were his chief subject for more than twenty-five years.

Monet designed an arched footbridge over the pond. Everyone called it the "Japanese bridge," and it was probably inspired by a bridge depicted in one of the Japanese prints that hung in his house. A screen of bamboo behind the other plantings reinforced the Japanese look of the garden. The turn of the century found Monet painting many views of the bridge.

Visitors to the garden remember a small rowboat moored to the bridge; perhaps Monet sat in it to get this head-on view. The bridge cuts across the canvas and extends beyond its edges. Above the bridge are weeping willow trees, which are reflected below in the water. In the foreground of the painting, the water lilies are large, but beyond the bridge they gradually become smaller, making them seem farther away.

Mingling with Nature

Monet was not interested in distinguishing the types of trees and plants that grew along the edges of the pond. The lilies and the reflections

40

Utagawa Hiroshige
INSIDE KAMEIDO TENJIN SHRINE

The bridge in Monet's garden was frequently compared to bridges in Japanese prints. The artist had avidly collected the designs of popular Japanese artists since 1870, and had even painted his dining room in two shades of yellow that one of his favorite Japanese artists used. He also planted flowers in his garden that he saw in prints, such as the wisteria in this print by the artist Hiroshige.

of the willows were what interested him. The floating leaves of the lily plants are painted a shimmering silver-green, reflecting brilliant sunlight. The flowers are indicated with large dabs of white paint, and with tinges of yellow and pink. The reflection of the bridge appears in deep red toward the bottom of the painting. Monet spoke of "peaceful meditation" and the Japanese idea of evoking "the whole by means of a fragment" when he talked about his paintings of his bridge at Giverny. Perhaps he wanted these canvases to set viewers' imaginations into action, building lovely gardens in their minds. He confessed that in his life he had "no other wish than to mingle more closely with nature."

THE HOUSES OF PARLIAMENT (EFFECT OF FOG)

The Houses of Parliament

In the fall of 1899, Monet traveled to London. When he was a young man he had painted the brand-new Houses of Parliament. Now, almost thirty years later, he painted them again. Rather than the buildings themselves, fog became the real subject of the series. The mists that rose from the river Thames and the soft vapors that replaced the sky obscured all the details of the architecture. Monet painted the towers as simple silhouettes. Of the water and the atmosphere, he created a rhapsody.

A Hovering Castle on a Phantom River

Monet made the Houses of Parliament float above the river like a hovering castle. He saw the massive government center as no more substantial than the rippling reflections of its towers in the river, which he painted with strokes of lavender and blue. Orange brightens the water and the sky above, with the setting sun burning through the fog. On the left, the horizon is blurred as sky and water become one veil of color. To balance this field of fog and water, the artist put his darkest and brightest colors on the right side of the canvas.

Paintings Salvaged at Last

This romantic scene was painted from Saint Thomas's Hospital, located directly across the river. Monet arranged for a room there to store his canvases and supplies. During the same visit to London, he painted views of the bridges that span the Thames. Each of his London canvases combined different effects of fog, light, and time of day. As the scene in front of him changed, he put aside one canvas and worked on another. When it was time to go back to Giverny, he was exhausted and not a single painting was finished.

In all, Monet worked on each canvas many different times. In spite of these efforts, he could not finish the paintings. "I ruined more than a hundred canvases," he confessed a year later. The atmosphere "kept changing all the time, and from one day to the next I could never find the same landscape." He salvaged some paintings and brought them back to his studio to work on for another year. Finally, in 1904, three and a half years after he began the series, Monet sent thirty-seven canvases to Paris to be seen together by the public.

Water Lilies

Water Landscapes

For the last twelve years of his life, Monet seldom left his home. The many Americans who came to learn about Impressionism from him made the village into a cosmopolitan artists' colony. But Monet ignored them, lost in his paintings. He had only one subject now— the gardens, and the lily pond, in particular. He called his paintings of the pond "water landscapes."

Monet painted this vibrant view of his aquatic garden when he was seventy-nine. It is different from his earlier landscapes. There is no sky and no horizon; no land shows, either, not even the edge of the pond. And the painting is twice as wide as his earlier ones. He had an assistant carry the six-and-a-half-foot canvas to the garden and set it up at a spot close to the water.

Monet wrote of his water lily series, "All day long I work on these canvases. I am brought one after the other." In his usual way, he tried to fix fleeting colors and to pin down a passing impression. He said he was "constantly at grips with nature." The trees and sky of his earlier days now existed for Monet only as reflections in the water. Lily leaves, some with rose-colored flowers, float gracefully across the pond, catching gold from the sun on their green surfaces.

Bearing Witness to the Universe

Late in his life, Monet embarked on the biggest project he had ever undertaken. He was painting a series of enormous water lily murals that were more than six feet high and twenty to fifty-five feet long. Today they line the walls of two large oval rooms in a museum in Paris called the Orangerie. Monet died in December of 1926. The murals, which were dedicated five months later, immortalize the lilies and Monet's very special way of seeing.

When students of art came to Monet for painting instruction, he usually turned them away. He felt words would not teach them; they should do what he did. If they followed him into the fields, as he had followed Boudin, a veil could be lifted from their eyes as it had been lifted from his. The lesson was to look hard and to attempt to capture an immediate impression. Monet himself looked so hard at nature all his life that as an old man he could see more than he had ever been able to see before. That is why the water landscapes became an entire universe to him and, through his brush, to others. Studying them is like following him and learning to see.

Up close, a section of one of Monet's water lily canvases looks like a modern abstract painting. Full of lively lines and patches of color, there is nothing that seems to represent the real world. Only from a distance do all the loose parts come together and become a light-drenched aquatic garden.

In 1920, Monet decided to dedicate his remaining years
to painting two murals of his beloved water gardens. For
this photograph, he stood in front of one of the segments
of the mural in a huge studio that was built for the job.
He did not live to see the paintings installed in two grand
oval galleries in the Orangerie in Paris, a museum where
millions of tourists and art lovers see them every year.
Looking at them is like gliding in a boat through Monet's
private world.

What Makes a Monet

Monet captured a particular moment, paying more attention to the overall impression than to a specific subject.

1.

2.

1. In the background, Monet defined only a few objects clearly.

2. Monet wove together an even web of color. He did not concentrate on any one area.

3. Monet rendered shadows and reflections with colors, not just with black.

4. Monet loved to paint water.

3.

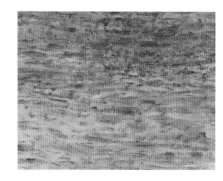

4.

a Monet?

RED BOATS, ARGENTEUIL